Tombeau of Ibn Arabi
and
White Traverses

ABDELWAHAB MEDDEB

Tombeau of Ibn Arabi
and
White Traverses

Translated by Charlotte Mandell

FORDHAM UNIVERSITY PRESS
NEW YORK 2010

Copyright © 2010 Fordham University Press

All rights reserved. No part of this publication may be reproduced, stored in a retrieval system, or transmitted in any form or by any means—electronic, mechanical, photocopy, recording, or any other—except for brief quotations in printed reviews, without the prior permission of the publisher.

Library of Congress Cataloging-in-Publication Data

Meddeb, Abdelwahab.
  [Tombeau d'Ibn Arabi. English]
  Tombeau of Ibn Arabi ; and, White traverses / Abdelwahab Meddeb ; translated by Charlotte Mandell.—1st ed.
    p. cm.
  Includes bibliographical references.
  ISBN 978-0-8232-3114-0 (cloth : alk. paper)
  ISBN 978-0-8232-3115-7 (pbk. : alk. paper)
  1. Meddeb, Abdelwahab—Childhood and youth. 2. Meddeb, Abdelwahab—Homes and haunts—Tunisia. 3. Meddeb, Abdelwahab. Tombeau d'Ibn Arabi. I. Jean-Luc Nancy. II. Mandell, Charlotte. III. Meddeb, Abdelwahab. Blances traverses du passé. English.

IV. Title. V. Title: White traverses.
PQ2673.E34T6613   2010
843'.914—dc22

2009030653

Printed in the United States of America
12 11 10   5 4 3 2 1
First edition

The works collected here were previously published in French as *Tombeau d'Ibn Arabi*, with drawings by Antonio Saura (Cognac: Fata Morgana, 1995), and *Blances traverses du passé*, with photographs by Jellel Gasteli (Cognac: Fata Morgana, 1997), later included in *L'Exil occidental*, (Paris: Albin Michel, 2005). Earlier versions of portions of the translations published here appeared in *Talus* (ed. Shamoon Zamir), *Notus* (ed. Pat Smith), *Parnassus* (ed. Herbert A. Leibowitz), *Boxkite* (ed. James Taylor), and *The Yale Anthology of French Poetry* (ed. Mary Ann Caws).

CONTENTS

vii Preface: On *Tombeau of Ibn Arabi*
     and *White Traverses*

  1 Tombeau of Ibn Arabi

 75 White Traverses

109 Afterword: Three Questions about
     Tombeau of Ibn Arabi
     JEAN-LUC NANCY

116 Notes

Preface

On *Tombeau of Ibn Arabi* and *White Traverses*

This *Tombeau* is not a question of praise or homage. It means to show how a text that maintains a link with the dead can be written at the present day. Of those dead, the living remember Ibn Arabi, who has never stopped speaking to us through the words that weave his phrases. From this privilege I draw another: his surprising closeness to Dante. They are the two symbolic figures who through history confirm my twofold spiritual genealogy, Arab and European, Eastern-Western. This duality requires going beyond creeds and polarities so that one ceases to be only from the West or only from the East (like the Koranic olive tree).

What becomes evident upon reading Ibn Arabi's *Tarjuman al-Ashwaq*[1] and Dante's *Vita Nuova* is the poet as interpreter of his own text, a text that places at the center of the poem the love inspired by the Lady: Niz'âm for one poet, Beatrice for the other.

With them is linked the name *Aya*, enriched by the long history of the exaltation of women by men, where the plurality of experiences remains marked by the singleness of the Name.

My own experiences are channeled by all this poetic memory into a singularity where certain pilgrimage sites between Paris and Carthage should be recognized, along with Italian (Siena, Florence, Rome), Andalusian (Ronda, Almeria), and Moroccan (the High Atlas) places, and other locations about which I will have to remain silent to preserve a measure of secrecy, mentioning only in passing the many deserts that appear throughout the stanzas—real deserts in Africa and Asia, the conventional desert brought to us by the first impressions of the early poetry of the Arabs before Islam, the desert of the room wherein the Mallarméan artifact gleams.

What else can I say about the foregrounding of the irregular (inherited both from Ibn Arabi and from Dante)? This irregularity becomes manifest through a prose haunted by alexandrines hidden between commas: in the flow of prose is hidden the elusive scansion of syllables. The twelve syllables that form the alexandrine get thrown off track, going under or over, for no other reason than to outwit the fixed count of syllables and to welcome the rule of the odd number. In this rhythmic scansion lives one of the mysteries of the comma, which has an unexpected usage, here deliberately rebellious to syntactic order, as if to signal by its mark the presence of a voice intended to give life to the poem. So the comma is the sign that, in the heart of the written text, there sounds the phantom of the spoken word. Know then that, from contraction to dilation, the breath, in its movements and its rest, will overflow grammatical logic. So the reader should know that these pages, in their fullness and their emptiness, ought to be heard according to listening to the discontinuous and to the discordant, as if to keep from glossing over whatever does not run smoothly in this world that absorbs us.

Here, evil and sickness are portrayed in all the theatricality of love. They nourish the attributes of beauty according to the role assigned to them by reality. And they are present only in themselves, without being driven away by the good. The duality of good and evil is here interlinked, with no loopholes or evasions. Here contraries are united according to a tension that varies from maximum to minimum.

Such a disposition is not the exclusive privilege of our orphan era, which, after Hölderlin, after Nietzsche, builds a tomb even for God. I see it even in the heart of previous eras. In truth, it remains lurking in the Unconscious of space and time. Revealed to me by frequent visits to the actual tomb of Ibn Arabi, a monument that still houses the ashes of the one who was born in Murcia in 1165 and died in Damascus in 1240. Situated in the Ayyubid neighborhood of Salihiyya, at the foot of Mount Qasyun, this Damascene tomb was rebuilt in the sixteenth century; in Ottoman fashion, its walls are decorated with glossy ceramic tiles where vegetal motifs drawn in blue stand out from a white background; but such supposedly floral motifs are transformed into masks of devils, surprisingly calling to mind the mannerist aesthetic called "grotesque." It is as if the eye emanating from the tomb were ordering us never to lose sight of the duty of looking evil in the face and converting it into what is peaceful. The serenity brought by laughter after the purification of tears.

And in the climate where I was born and grew up, on the African coast that looks toward Europe while being lapped by the waves of the Mediterranean, it is white that is dreamed pure. So it was necessary to short-circuit the current that feeds the myth. In the heart of this crossroads were captured the effluvia that inspired *White Traverses*. Here again contraries were confirmed by the truth of their coincidence. From the primeval scene appeared visions teaching us that the impure lodges in the pure. Another poetic horizon welcomed the thought emanating from experiences in the century that ancient writings corroborate through an ethics that can take the negative into account without ever needing to abolish it.

This is the good fortune of one who has been able to take hold of the course of things by experimenting with two sequences of history animated by conjunctures quite far apart, at two very different speeds. This is because my childhood in Tunis in the 1950s authorized me to frequent a world that still bore within it archaic vestiges that resonate with what I chance to grasp from ancient or medieval texts. On our African shore, we were anthropologically the contemporaries of Euripides, of Raymond Lull. A decade later, a sidereal time carried us far away, as if to discover ourselves entirely in what migrated from America to reconfigure all the lands of the Earth.

Tombeau of Ibn Arabi

I

Ruins, remember, neglected grounds, dust, wanderers' refuge, the voice blends with its echo, look at the man in the cave, the rock is a mirror, everything is deserted, I wait for the clouds to shed their tears, I wait for the flowers to speak, I call out, no one answers, the stone hears my excitement, how many moons thrown in the well, how many suns come out of oblivion, the tree touches the sky, and the spark spells out a star, lightning flashes a carpet in the shadows, on the headlands in the south, winds brush against the thunder, on the path, I say a rosary of pearls, black camels double the mounts and hills, sand covers my tracks in the dunes, seers wandering in the shade of gardens, the summer heat is a woman's smile that unearths the custom of the dolls, so many vague paths, oh memory, oh mystery, the light appears fleeting, inside the heart an ancient feeling is engraved, which separates.

II

With what words to say, in what bush to set foot, in peace, in danger, overwhelmed with love, to run back in one's tracks.

III

She withdrew as soon as she appeared, she brought with her her perfumes and her spices, at the dawn of peacocks, forget the hour, the throne in the vision is dazzling, sashay the lady on a crystal floor, she lifts up her dress, she is a sun that revives the colors of the day, her fragrance brings joy, her ankle jingles with silver, her legs tremble with each step, she sends missives to thirsting peoples, mount of the nomad, home of the passerby, when she offers you intimacy, she opens herself up to your memory, and snatches you from the law, in one night, she initiates into the hidden, and abolishes the rites that check desire, in every famous court, in every temple, she is the glory of every book, in vain I called at her leaving, pile after pile, my patience runs dry, I preserve her beauty, which blazes at the most extravagant of my travels, and in me the angel's shiver spreads.

IV

Hello nostalgic one, orphan, friend buried in the fabric of pain, come back to the resonant light which, from its source, gushes forth, you, the recluse, who consecrate your fasting, your penitence, your effort, your seasons, now you leave the hermitage, you emerge from your wintering, don't back away on the day of the meeting, don't skirt round the canopy bed, where the curtains fall soft, altar that smells of the entrails, near the lake that mirrors the blue of the sky, your heart is a burning lamp, you throw a handful of live coals, your throat cadences the pulsing water that, out of rock, rises up, and you who lead the docile camels, lower the flag next to the stela, there, at the crossroads, stop at the bend in the road, rest an hour and say hello, before you go toward the red domes that appear in the distance, on the horizon of fever, hello nostalgic one, orphan, tearful one, if they answer your greeting, may your gift be of beauty, if they say nothing, continue on your journey, cross the river, don't speak to the group, to the tribe, pass through the white tents that throw their shadows on salty lips, and hail the lovers all, Judith and Aya, Hind or Hera, ask them to show you the way, brilliant white, sparkling between the peaks.

V

Welcome her who descends among you, whom fine gold dust blinds, which she scatters in passing, she stops, before she opens the closed door, while the night drops her black veils, and you say to her, welcome, elegant one, stranger, subtle in love, in your name, I enter into bliss, captive in the fortress of your desire, I am your target, your arrows puncture me, on the smooth stone I shine my hands, she shows her bare arms, lightning splits the deepest part of the night, she says, what more does he want, am I not the icon that never deserts his heart, isn't it enough to contemplate me, in any place, at any hour?

VI

She interrogates me in the knot of desire, and accuses me, homeless, from desert to desert, scattered, I go from one extreme to its opposite, strewn scraps, time doesn't put me back together, what's to be done, without harmony, show the way, you who magnetize me, don't saturate me with reproaches, tall flames rear up, tears course down my cheeks, the exile is different when he comes back, he has trouble walking in an empty labyrinth, no home will stay inhabited, when it is seized, in the revolution of dark nullity.

VII

At night you see sorrow sting, it lives at the very bottom of the heart, I said to them, where can one find the ones who've left, they answered, they have chosen to stay, there where the emanations of infinity smell sweet, I tell the wind, go join them where they rest, in the shade of that tree, the one that is neither east nor west, bring them the thought of the disconsolate one, carrying the tatters of separation.

VIII

And I was jostled by some ladies, come from far away to visit the holy places, they encircled me, they shaded me from the sun, they told me, be ready, take off your shoes, learn to live the second that your breath leaves your body, how many men have they made holy this way, by suggesting that they run, on a field of coals, joining the branches of the valley, reeling in the shimmering noon, crossing the huge swarm of insects, that cover the hillsides with their hordes, you know don't you, that beauty ravishes man, and carries him off in the tornado, that despoils, I would find you at the destined time, beyond the infernal valley, there, behind the mausoleum, whose high dome defies the arid chaos, there where they keep watch, the ones who have tasted ecstasy, close to women, who exude ambergris and musk, and who, shy, free their hair, somber drapes, behind which they hide their faces.

IX

Their youth is no more, their tracks have been erased, their site deserted, but their passion, inside their bodies, stays new forever, such are their traces, such are their regrets, in their memory, hearts melt, I cried out to her while she strutted about, you whose beauty is the only good, see how I have nothing left, I've stained my face with black spots, do not despair of love, when he might stop breathing, he who is drowning in his word, and who burns in the fire of exile, you who stir up the flames, don't lose patience, our bodies will learn how to cross the devouring furnace.

X

Lightning slices the thread of vision, the chest echoes the voice of the thunderbolt, the stormclouds wander above the orchards, before the downpour soaks the trees, the water falls hard, and hurtles down the slopes, the earth exhales its breeze, mixed with the essence of flowers, and wood, and leaves, the body is impregnated with such fleeting smells, and the hand and the soul build glass walls, which let the light fall red, as if to make crimson the black desert vipers, moving at the feet of the white ladies, seated, frontal, hieratic, large eyes quick to unveil, generous, tender, humble in their greatness.

XI

When a child, I remember, there was a woman, from my window, every day, I saw her, she didn't leave her garden, she didn't stop contemplating her beauty, she rambled between the beds of tulips and irises, from that, I'm not surprised, the woman I saw then, is a mirror that carried the image of my future mistress.

XII

Ashen doves of the Comoros, your song brings the smells of the tropics, it purifies the breeze, and multiplies pains, your cooing tells of sobs, funereal voices, cease your melancholy recitations that breathe in from dawn to sunset, and like an echo, sighs of the nostalgic and petitions of the forsaken, in unison we chanted the threnody, at the foot of a dry tree, and the wind spread another lament, which woke desire in us, light reaching us from beyond the mountains, night covered with dew, we shared our fruits, she sauntered round me, pagan idol, she sang, countertenor, an episode from the Passion, she piled up, in a circle, long flat stones, she invited me to kiss them, to touch them, to such ex-votos she proclaimed her avowal of faith, lips against lips, the fires of our bodies lured a bestiary, the red antelope, the black-and-white heifer, tinged with henna, their eyes, at night, invented in the middle of the desert, a meadow where they gamboled, before coming back luxuriant, to the enclosure of our enchanted garden, it was the night of transformation, forms shifted and changed, and I felt able to welcome them all, I saw myself wandering through lands, mumbling all languages, handling all writings, entering and exiting, according to chance meetings, going from one scene to another, marveling at the vestiges of peoples, traveling at times, erratic, moving, changing, in the mirror of metamorphoses, at the mercy of passion which runs the world.

XIII

Naked, lying on the ground, vague and empty, after the voyage of inner vision, back in the world, present, without taking action, I saw a changing procession, the horse, in slow motion, ran behind the sloping neck of the bison, mask of the buffalo, then bull, the image resists naming, expanding ostrich, flying sea turtle, corrupt vulture camel-humped, slow blue coincidences, which stretch out smoking, on the screen of my eyes, the sky is the backdrop for shadows, at the height of twilight, the caravan rises, and enters, by the balcony, the desert, at the time of the first stars, tracks captured by the mirrors of the cold, behind the windowpanes, streams a winter light, frail sounds, flowers that pierce the weft of noise, veils of insomnia in the city.

XIV

I walked in the maze of morning, winter shepherd, watching out for the circle of wolves, the jet-black bird was singing on the obsidian, black on black, night hadn't left the day, I tricked the subsoil, companion of subways, the lion, guardian of the square, lay dormant on his pedestal, the merry-go-round of cars, dragons spitting fire from their nostrils, my head wound tight in marsh sounds, the nerves laid bare, mirror of the heart, an archer took aim at the clock, on the front of the train station, in the square the beautiful young woman appeared, draped in a golden shawl, scarlet sari, of the caste of love, her braided hair struck her hips, and sounded a noon, which seemed like midnight, I invited her to drink a light Loire wine, brisk and peppery, her long fairy hands, set with rings, were reflected in the ruby wine dress, the smell of sulfur pressed us, to visit the blue rooms, in the palace of the edicts, I saw a white stain, behind the veil of quicksilver, where the eye, bitter varnish, gave sheen, that woke, teeming, the desert track, alchemy of dust, on the immaculate page, the caravan awaited my arrival, to give birth to the wonders of the world, ores from Africa, Andean masks, busts from China, stelae from Arabia, scents from the islands, Tartar parchments, under the languid weight of palm trees, opening one's eyes, the aircraft flew over the city, unmoving shadows, in the milky skies, the gulls, on yellow waves, drifted far from the gray shores.

XV

Climb step by step the stairs, from the top, examine the abandoned monasteries in the desert, marble columns, partly standing, pediments in ruins, gazelles graze there, slender, fragile, wary, fearful, veins trembling under skin, film of sweat, it is a feverish morning, you bear allegiance to the sky, in the brilliance of day, the movement of the stars appears to you, you are the guardian of a perennial garden, you thwart the changing of the seasons, you read with naked eye the invisible in the heavens, and you save the gazelles, from the wounding teardrops, and you will not deny the word, that one of them posed to her fellow creatures, at night, she said to them, we are the erased faces of the sun, our hidden whiteness, gives light, like foam, elusive firefly, which goes out on the milky breast, barely covered, in the shadow of the branches, trembling openwork of foliage, which project their chiaroscuro, on the bed of the illuminated garden, by our furtive smiles, lightning in the night.

XVI

Black day, rain beats on the windowpane, the weeping angels come to you, they sing the glory of the absent one, wave after wave, the inspiration inside overwhelms me, and I cannot repeat what I hear, the jealous voice stops at the threshold of speech, the angel musicians blow into their long trumpets, and chase the rain, you go through the clouds, balls of cotton, and you find the sun again, above the metallic vault, lunar soil, depending on the pressure, the cabin vibrates, and straightens out its long quills and remiges, the angels' music pierces through the steel jet engines, from the porthole, *putti* aim at me, blond curls, their tears stream down, the soul forms in them, unstable, into what does it incarnate, it might enter into stone, inanimate, unnamed, I recognize it inside the heart, in the beloved's tears, remains only regret, for her, obscure, I went closer, our meeting celebrated loss, and anxiety, between the two of us, marched, sentinel that now appeared, now disappeared, deep inside me a burn shone, grain of sand that wounds the eye, the tribe invited us to eat, but the burn prevented me, the tents of goods were overflowing, the vision dulled the appetite, the gazelle would rather die, than be caught in the trap, I hid my tear, I walked straight between the men, I listened in secret to the image contained in the heart, the crow flew over us, landed on the antenna, cawed and beat his wings, black voice I couldn't revoke, I left the grounds in haste, driving at the foot of the sun, to the rhythm of the stones, I said, never, to such a desert, will I return, and here I am going back by the heavens, separation doesn't interrupt love it kills, sing the angels, in absence, beauty doesn't tarnish, wherever it is present, it remains as it is, unchangeable in thought.

XVII

Light irradiates the sunrise, day appears, it is a revelation, the west stays dark, near the full moon, pale pastille, in the flow of night, the dawn mists dissipate, brightness that turns you away from buildings, which perpetuate a memory of death, on such symbols, runs the east wind, murmur of strange message, beyond torment, beyond affliction, taste of ecstasy, which happens after the seething within, drunkenness carries away the mind, in front of a round moon, which sinks in a trail of blood, on the opposite side the sun is rising, such harmony burns, against your chest her breast heaves, mingled breaths, you doze off, and the day grows, and the east wind stirs up the bodies' fire, or extinguishes it, in union, to dwell in the beloved, between survival in the igneous traces, and instant annihilation, ash raised by the wind, in gusts, above the silvery waters of the river.

XVIII

She crosses the oval square, theater in a shell, golden reflections on green damask, bodies find their nature again, bath of red clay, at the edge of the fountain, the hot water burns, the oratorio, in its last movement, gives rhythm to the exchange of elixirs, bodies fallen into the Name, *die before dying*, enter into the shadow of the All-Power, then return to life, scarlet faces, blood and breath spin quickly in the body, at dawn, the youth wears his silk vestment, corundum intaglios, robe like evening, at the sapphire hour, tents raised, we get ready to leave, nocturnal voyage, stars trace the path, in the shelter of the region of day, in the excess of senses, not being able to move, drooling, eyes bulging, gone out of myself, seeing me other, in the spectacle of calm pain, no one dares come near, beyond the principle, which demands to be kept in, vertigo in the heart, how to face her, her eyes snarl an authoritarian music, the sonorous attraction of the planets crushes my ears, I drink her in, I am so thirsty, vessel without steering, that the waves toss, right yourself, be master of your body, cover yourself with veils, speak to her behind screens, don't contemplate her face-to-face, go into yourself, in separation, wait for the morning visitors, and those of midnight, air yourself in the shelter of their wings, with a thousand touches, welcome the furtive vision that, after the instant of blindness, adds sharpness to sight, to awaken you to the cries of crows, noisy black characters, inscribed between the abyss and the heavens, jet-black proclamation flying over the white camels, on the edge of the desert, empty space, flat earth, rough, steppe where black sounds write themselves.

XIX

With automatic palanquins, human-size dolls, masts tip over, in search of the sea, on the stretch of desert, field of fossils, cavities and moon furrows, lights and sounds, the pact seals the hearts, the deed tricks, she offers me a grappa of black grapes, the tears held back excite the storm, the interior sun is covered, the bitter gullet, capital of the gift, on the outskirts of a rusted land, where to face the danger, and deposit my income, and see her face in every thing, in the darkness, in the light, in obstacle, in transparency, and wear the mask and the veil, which doesn't prevent one from seeing, from leaving to beginning, or moving complicated through the world, the bird of prey flies over the cliff, that gives wings to the spice tree, the sap stings the gum till it bleeds, within reach of finery, in the quiet night, the recluse moans, pebbles loosen the vast square, footsteps crunch in the jealous night, language gets lost, regular of the night, your form liquefies, incandescent lava, which congeals as it goes by, dark temple, where we hear the ritual fragments, languages inside out, after forty nights, come, knock on the door, cross the patio, enter the tombs, go by the oblong room, go down the seven steps, I'll wait for you in back of the garden, in the hut, near the greenhouse, don't speak to the old guard, undress yourself, wear the loincloth the *OM* adorns, don't repeat anything from memory, wet your lips with new words, articulate the sound of inspiration, don't translate the meaning, so that the scansion is thirst in you, cover the stages of refusal, let go your cry to the animal echo, shepherd of stars, nocturnal cup bearer, between the two of us passion speaks, wine flows, I keep watch with the one, who goes to sleep beneath lightning, she closes her eyes, and falls asleep with the dead, then she is reborn, wine's sister, who refreshes sight, upon the meeting the sun, the late moon, harbor of the senses.

XX

And you who wander, don't proceed quickly, pay court to rest, time is fixed in the track, stop there, look closely at the wrinkles of the relief, straighten your sleeves, listen to the sharp cry, knead the silt that fashions bodies, how I would like to set foot, in that which happens to thought, but the foot does not follow, scold the voice, the singing exercise is corrupted, if it doesn't inspire song, change direction, turn to the right, on the banks of the valley, you will find her again, in silence, in dialogue, in rupture, in return to silence, around a people, who await nothing, engraved in the heart of misery, would I be a stranger, among the goitrous, led astray on the red soil, from such a high valley, where water streams, among the green shocks of hair, at the boundary of earthen castles, with eagle niches, alone in the country of mules, in search of the unknown woman, who spells my name, on the threshold of departures?

XXI

Empty homes, windows torn away, gray of the sky, devastated neighborhood, Sunday of nothing, expatriate heads, between the ruined corridors, and the walled-up doors, language of Babel, which cut the being in two, walking in the shadow of myself, on the lookout for a mirage, on the horizon of a noble modesty, passing unperceived through the hedges of crime, on the poster of the hospital, with red bricks, on the sermon sign, on the steam fabric, color of diseases, that the chimneys spit out, absence of self, on the way that leads to a drink, *eau de vie*, which heals cracks on the lips, between the dirty children, and the cardboard suitcases, broken lamps, on the routes through the city, the hot wind disfigures, sparks of sand slicing, energy of fission, the melting of train stations, deliquescent rails, beneath bridges, tall towers collapsed, the incandescent air burns the intestines, the city is captured, by indecipherable wretches, sulfurous smell, which holds the throat captive, the view sweeps over the bunghole, over the eye of the needle, my face, a flare that changes speed, mountain color, that the sea wind shades, under what rubble to restore it, in what forgetfulness to speak to it, of wood or of stone, on the paths outside the walls, toward a desert that welcomes me, at camels' pace, the dogs bark in the darkness, the hearth affixes the sign of the beloved, on the walls of night sitting without moving, in the heart of ardent cacti, coming out of the apocalypse, I warm myself at her fire, and pet the speckled lion cubs, which surround her.

XXII

I listen to her, who has no voice, in search of the rest, the seasons pass, the houses go to ruin, I was in a good mood, before scowling, the vast plain narrowed, between the columns, things grew, without my knowing, I was not the guard, I would have hunted them down, between the celebration and the business deal, I spat, I sat down on the rugs, which hide the cracks in the floor, our shadows are engulfed, in empty homes, peacocks open the day, bodies flit about, next to souls, between brightness and clouds, the vaults do demivolts, at the cry of the lovers, desire stirs, between the white tombs, banners laid down, on the hill.

XXIII

I see my heart beat, in a jar, my cheeks bleed, between the two worlds, the tree is a miniature, which awakens the shades, in the lap of a playful girl, round immaculate dresses, my body, in each pore, hollows out, I receive the visit of the sun, a garden grows, in my toe, beauty swells, in the cube of youth, the alma rises, at night, she offers me her body, haughty, I lay her down on the bed of my disease, in the hollow of a room, high and narrow, in the clamor of hieroglyphs, ants, coleopterans, birds of prey, tiara, sickness has clothed me, in white alabaster, it is a gash, which has made me a frightful sight, I feel her scarlet vulva, the gold of her chain coils up on my black pubis, it is a fire that illuminates, in back of the tomb, the face coated with butter, the reified air, in the silence, I hear the noise of bodies, peace dawns, she smells the coagulated blood, which captures my disease, convalescence begins, I tear up the picture, carried next to my heart, I unbutton the suit, which binds my torso, the sun strikes, free and constrained, I dig out the soft clay, a blue chemistry colors my voices, I transcribe the love letter, I invent a pulpit, behind the veil, hiding the one who, in my illness, loses her way, daughter of a bloodthirsty king, I sneeze, and the breath strikes the vertebra, which burns, she comes to me, sure of her beauty, complexion of straw-colored wine, she sparkles with a fugitive spirit, intoxicated, I undress her, the stars go out, between the wound and the caress, I return to illness, which her lips increase.

XXIV

Taffeta, sound of the sea, the cypress is a candle, in which green hair burns, the mountain is a camel, it unloads its burden, steps resound on the flagstones, and ricochet off the clouds, I invite her on the journey, in the shade of the fig tree, opposite the isthmus, which is a barrier, where the spirit sinks, before the jetty, awaiting the ferry, lurking in the open sea, at the edge of the storm, the sea sends back its waves, the stars linger to arrange the dawn, the seagull is an island coming near, the mast is a tree groaning, she rises, with the day, she looks through the porthole, she washes in the foam, she covers herself with azure, which rekindles her whiteness.

XXV

The survivors of the sleepless night, gather pebbles and pearls, at the rising of the dawn, the banner of night floats away, the day-blind people leave the day, morning is an eagle, decorated with letters, eloquent people, scribes of desire, the foreigner wears the sign of the fish, in the folds of the burn, up there, he waits to die, in a desolate landscape, the water flows on a bed of knives, the fetid smell assails the visitor, who haunts the black night, insomniacs publish a morning musk, drunk, the branches bend under the breath of the those who walk by night, wretched, thoughtless, yearning without object, shipwrecked in the cry.

XXVI

On forgotten tracks, in unnamed places, I see the chorus of mourners, on the south banks, I look at homes in ruin, in the cool morning, I admire her, who wears the mask of pain, the dead cross the black footbridge, and pluck the fruits of silence, the rain crisscrosses the gray light, I said, yes, I'll come, without ruse, or shield, that's how I replied, to her who spoke, with a cut heart, hunted, without cover, on the plain, the four winds brought contradictory messages, she says, I will divide myself, I will be new, like the sun, each day.

XXVII

On the page of the sacrificed animal, the mihrab sings in the interior, the fire, that is devouring in my breast, is a twilight, fed by the evening musk, the moon jostles the branch, the seed splits the face, the fruit breaks open, the star bores into a tomb, pain is a book, which grips my skull, the sun leaves my belly, the sky reddens the shadows, the stage is empty, the crown breaks, the corners murmur, on a crystal floor, the wind brushes the craftsman, who gathers a fistful of sand, his hands crumble, the stone turns, in this yellow world, desire is a dome, that collapses, in the fog of fever, my sweaty body, back again in the desert, covets the solitude of the two sisters, whom my senses, clothe, in white.

XXVIII

I take the path, that leads to the garden of error, I play with names, behind the grove of truth, I drink where the child gathers up his dice, I hide in the thicket, where the gazelle trembles, the wolf drowns the shepherd's song, a breeze dusts my body, in the black day, the downpour fills the lake, that separates the two countries, in a Sumerian goblet I drink a wine preserved, in an amphora of clay, buried underground, for millennia, the ancient goblet, fossil from paradise, gives off a breath, that I scent as deadly.

XXIX

I wandered, lost, won, I laugh, cry, alone, in the road, exulting, in the practice, keeping watch, in the morning, at rest, after movement, I drop the bridle, unearth the roots, drained of blood, I cross uncertainty, eyes open, I wreathe the nightmare, from my spittle, I pull out the thread, which unravels my body, my form disappears, my soul remains, outside of its carcass, in the prison of cause, which abrogates sight, I walk on filth, palpable in my nothingness.

XXX

The vision brings white smells, which send back forms, and envelop them in Esparto grass, at the foot of a tree, whose fruits I pick, without eating them, I see the silver filament of the nascent moon, I am afraid of being annihilated, I touch smooth stone, lying on the ground, star, neighbor of day, may my eye not be torn out, may I read the obverse of my entrails, the flames devour me, the sand attacks my eyes, and stops in my throat, I can't breathe, or speak, I am burned, I go back to my palace, dazed, on moon paths, I travel, with a white step, which weakens the ground, I suffocate in armor, from another time.

XXXI

Foreigner in her homeland, tattooed, crimson, viper bites, scorpion stings, have anaesthetized her body, traitress, messenger, she pulls back, then gives herself, she returns sight to the blind, and drags her veils, proud, decked with finery, I contemplate her, and wander, she laughs, she is the beauty of the hour, naked, she forbids chatter, on a balcony, I touch her, her skin, all silk, is a gift, which captures the soul, she tells the secret to man, magic is in her hands, she covers herself, and the heart breaks, she wets her lips, her eyes fool me, she offers me a throne on water, her body eclipses the lunar disc, the east wind lifts her skirt, between two states, with the analogy, I bear witness, with the limited word, furtive, she buries a trace, that I recognize in the effort, fever strikes the stone, I walk in the mud, toward the unknown, I throw myself, feet bare, into the cold valley, I pursue her emaciated body, with some latecomers, on which the desert closed, her chest shone in the shadow, panther eyes, that kindle my desire, I circumambulate a cube, stamped by the lunar seal, I meet her, thirsting, she erases the sign of day, and plunges me into night, she laughs, noisily, she leaves me perplexed, a bewildered ghost, playing on the edge of the precipice.

XXXII

She has an arched back, she walks on shadows, which dance, idle, she de-louses herself, recluse in the fog, she watches a gaggle of migrating birds pass, on the river's bank, on the side of the mountain, there is a destroyed village, surrounded by grottos, rooms for the djinn, my body is a protruding stone, I visit fever, on the day of rest, she has left, without my knowing, I see a bed in the lake, in which her face is mirrored, I sink into her image, in search of her people, scattered to the winds, my body is cut, from downstream upstream, I let myself be guided, by the jujube tree at the end, I meet some idols, at the break in the wormwood, where I embalm my diseases, the saints walk on their wounds, pain is a hole, it blackens my reflections, I suffocate, I find her again, in the reality, of her embroidered lace, I open her blouse, I drink from her navel, I enter absence, I bear allegiance to her, I sign her wrist, with a metal of nocturnal glimmers, it burns flowers, save the narcissus and the tulip, she offers me a cowl, it has the emblem of the scorpion, the rough wool electrifies my body, dense in the night, crumbly like coal, her hair is a hive, which hums around a captive queen, Arab and white, she speaks frankly, with a Latin flavor, she hides her body, and uncovers it, she lets down her hair, and gathers it up, the things of the day take shape, in the unfinished clay, with sculptor's hands, I touch the black stone, the mark opens, like a window, the night sparkles, the moon is a plate, which I break, and bury, under the circle of fire.

XXXIII

The whole town is talking about it, I call for her help, and tremble, she says, put up at the house of him who is proud, to receive you, and place yourself high up, stay there a long time, don't lavish advice, on him who can't hear, injustice is to give, to him who doesn't know how to take, full and soft, she enflames my senses, her speech is a smell, which renders crimson, wherever it goes, on peaks, or lower down, she lifts me up, I call for her, she excavates the treasure, which was sleeping in me, her presence peoples ruins, like a mirage, I taste her spirit's trace, her light irradiates the gray room of my body, her features visit other forms, she crushes the seed of the heart, bitter smell, abrupt landscapes, sharp smoke, the city congeals, from the window, I examine the world, which kills.

XXXIV

With short strides, accelerated step, ancient, she profanes her youth, desire rises up in her, she burns the seventy veils, she smells the flower of age, she climbs the three steps, she disappears into the skies, she comes down, I shut myself in with her, her body is a lamp, which lights up forty nights.

XXXV

The hoopoe sways, on the tree beyond the world, the voice sighs, and cries, spirits separate from bodies, the breath extinguishes, I drink in ecstasy, my passion is in the unveiling, I leave the darkness, where I was prisoner, I bear witness, prostrate myself, the voice is a noise, in the city, glass quivers, autumn scorches, fire devours.

XXXVI

Black, in black eyes, clouds cover the peaks, the grotto is a sleeping dragon, the seconds are shadows, that tremble, in black eyes, son of the epic, I hurtle down the paths, at the speed of lightning, I cross the guarded estate, I desecrate the village, I carry away the beloved, I enter the black, of her black eyes.

XXXVII

Three shades pass, they dazzle in the night, they assassinate, they attract, as the flame does the moth, they veil their faces, to spare the weak, they have a slow hand, they throw black cats, into spiders' webs, they speak in a loud voice, they are visiting, in a country, where they establish a house, to welcome the wanderers, who celebrate beauty, among a destitute people, only the poor enter, who unwind the irony of the moment.

XXXVIII

I travel in the world, which is a dark night, I visit fifty cities, where solitude begins, ends, phantom cities, ruined neighborhoods, new squares, in the heavens, with the angels, I tremble at the lightning, I am dizzy, in air pockets, fever is a machine, which doesn't stop, in the black night, I walk at the pace, of an empty spirit, that, in the darkness, sees and does not think.

XXXIX

She opens my eyes, my ears, she touches my nostrils, she submerges me in water, in the shade of the tent, she says, do not feel trapped, look at me face-to-face, I am as confused as you, don't sit down, where the embers blossom, names are the traces of our sharings, don't gather together the red twigs, don't throw them, where those who are near, halt, carry the salvation of lovers, bashful, at the limit of themselves, delicate, in the trial, that prevents them from feeling the golden vessels, the silk clothes, crime, penitence, on the road leading to the wood, of their dream.

XL

Like conquerors, unable to return, in a foreign country, I see myself in every thing, the heart vast, like a third-world country, inaccessible, I contract, I dilate, one step into death, and return, I accept, I decline, she trusts me with signs, which I interpret, when her eyelashes bat, lover, whose look kills, her speech has the secret of fire, in solitude, after obstacle, earthen walls, sepulcher for the old world, which the sun enamels, the musician changes key, the migrants dance, morning birds, in a meager spring, fistfuls of insects, in the voluptuousness of the distant land.

XLI

The white vipers of the desert, play in corners and stones, they leave tracks, in the labyrinth, that the one lost on the trail spots, in the night, which does away with fingers and toes, the stars gather together their sparks, in a solar hearth, which lights up the inner abyss, of all, I have loved her, who sits enthroned, perfect and hidden, I cross the veils, that adorn her, my eyes become blind, not one piece of dust dulls her, she tears up the darkness, like a piece of paper, she cries in the night, her hair is a curtain, which falls on the crime, at full noon.

XLII

Late she rises, in her bed, she lazes, she hears the olive tree sing, she celebrates man, frail and lithe, she is as old as the moon, she is full as a reed, she doesn't weigh the days, she doesn't stay in huts, where the self grows and wanes, her right armpit is a dawn, that shines, her pubis swallows the bleeding sun, she is naked, her fingers sprout water, her skin is a shiver, she anoints her body with oil, she peddles sea salt, her wet eyes are grasshoppers, that leap toward the desert, which I open to her after a luxury, that defies the apparent privation.

XLIII

The white bird from Yemen comes down into the garden, and wakes up its fellows, who live in the giant araucaria pine, its shadow covers the orange grove, the flowers raise their spears to the sky, dawn makes the temples of night tremble, and tears them apart, by pulling at the white thread that appears at the horizon, it takes out a fairy, who opens my chest, and washes my heart, it is black magic, daughter of night, who goes in hunt of the tempestuous bird, I flee, as soon as the day triumphs, the embers inside the liver crackle, hell lights up, at the death of the stars, the sun climbs the ladder of the equator, I search through the remains, I call out, nothing reaches me, I don't look back, the smell casts a gloom over my way, I don't unseal the moon, which by day, guides my steps, where the paths fork, the angels bring a sudden cloud, rain submerges the valley, the flood carries off my things, the shepherd of clouds chases the storm away, the white bird from Yemen perches, on a two-horned height, that has the sticky color of mud, it hinders the fairy who wanted to use me, at nightfall.

XLIV

I collide with a passerby, I am in the clouds, my head is cut, I wander between high and low, I walk in the sun, without seeing the sun, I keep pace with the herd, I place, between their hands, my turbaned head, my light streams, with my blood, poor among them, stripped, only breath is left in my body, I am ready to die, standing, in front of the beautiful Arab woman, whose Latin voice, sets galloping, the arid contours, the white porous stone set into a bestiary, I stop where the things from above, incarnate as a presence, which is an image, jealous of my ignorance, she covers her face, and adds to my passion, I die twice, to others, to myself, only to be close to her, a promise unites us, at sunset, the enemy, a plausible double, carries me away from her, I am feverish, I take shelter in the houses of absence, the angels of the night come down, into my heart, and turn in my veins, to the slow rhythm, of my garish urges.

XLV

Being would be nothing, if sometimes presence didn't become a lady, dressed in black, piercing the vowel of absence, which I recognize, profuse, in the language, and the world, when even it could adorn the rat, the cat, the ass.

XLVI

I will not forget the day, when I wasn't able to be equal to the greatness, which presented itself to me, it was a day, when I admired, those who succeeded, seeing them was a medicine, my spirit rose at their desire, my stay, among them, was long, from the day, the bird flew *à destre*, their house was prosperous, despite the meager years, the mountain path, flattened at their feet, and the arid deserts threw into their ears, the echoes of water, they are idols, who helped me come near, and who didn't deign to guard, those who offered them, on a plate, their smitten hearts.

XLVII

I bite into the colocynth, I break the stem of the euphorbia, my heart, like a fettered eagle, doesn't attain its flight, be patient, she tells me, your time will come, you will rejoin me, don't hurry, how can I wait, I tell her, the prisoner is a rebel, patience is an exile, that I don't trap, the smoke evaporates, she appears, with her secret banner, the white of her eye is a cloud, which the narcissus stains, she is sitting, upright, on the throne, she spins round and round, her orb pierces the blindness, that precedes being, the illusion doesn't give it outline, it is a plaything, that my memory melts, on the scene of the gaze, word doesn't name her, thought doesn't conceive of her, she comes near, she moves away, she creates a jealousy, that whips my blood, she haunts me, like a chimera, I wash my eyes, I reach out my hand, the veils burn, I see her, I touch her.

XLVIII

A lump of wax, as the night goes by, her alveoli are letters, that bore into the book, the honey, that drips from it, is an inspired word, stammered by her, who has brown lips, and full legs, which tremble at every step, her absence makes the face crimson, the clarity of her teeth is a white page, light, between life and death, she penetrates the home of leisure, she tramples on the garden of full hearts, she listens to the wavelength of flowers, I call the winds, that carry the sun, on the cheeks of the friend, the answer is short, like the mark the wind erases, as soon as it is imprinted, on the cold sand, of the sleepless night.

XLIX

The moon, in front of me, bows down, the crow at night flies over, the paths of exile, which lead to the western nations, I walk, on the white shroud, that covers the soil, the inner images dry in the wind, I erase the letters, that I wrote, on hidden notebooks, to the closest friend of the heart.

L

Time is limited, my body is empty, I travel, in the moonlight, I carry man's pact, I have the bitter taste of the remedy, I wait to be cured, she passes in front of my door, like a fugitive, she is a flash of lightning, which throbs, and signals its irony, above the shoulder of my pain, she is a veil, which I lift, to raise myself to pity, which was unknown to me, I tame the wild beast, that is in me, so as not to perish, faced with the slave-recluse, in her white fever, daughter of the lamp, that lights up the face of the guest, who knocks at night, and asks for rest, she is a sleeping pearl, in the hollow of its shell, waiting for the diver, who would reveal it to the light.

LI

Like from far away, a mirage in the desert, like the sun, which blesses the morning of a great house, she appeared, face uncovered, I had called her, behind the veil of fever, when I was lost, in a hostile steppe, drunk, in a shoreless ocean, when I had come back, horseman with a burned face, I saw her pass, between her eyebrows, a flame was budding, through the crack that separates her teeth, I entered the vision, she was living in an isolated orchard, with a dove, which flew, and came back, with no other partner, since I crossed the sea, I invite her in thought, and rub against her intact solitude.

LII

Like a viper, risen from under the stones, that one's foot moves, she bites, without waiting, and by surprise, she wears the mask of mystery, and surrounds you with softness, in her arms, you dissolve, and you fall into illness, wherever she takes you from, you are finished.

LIII

I find peace again, which those who rise into the heavens meet, I cross the great ruse, veiled in bliss, the windows of amber, and of musk, affix their seal, on our tyrannical hearts, which propose onerous pacts, difficult to honor, despite the equal pleasure, that we've shared, in the distinction.

LIV

I adapted to a climate, that is not mine, where I breathed the moist ocean air, and built a square house, of glass, opening out onto a land of rock, cut by electric wire, stretched between two wooden posts, on which, I hung my heart, lighthouse showing the way, to those who leave, and to those who mourn for them, I rest in my home, after years of travel.

LV

She incarnated, between the two sexes, sometimes girl, sometimes boy, we held each other tight, one against the other, like the two letters, that are mirrored in my name, we were then no more than one, we who are two, she would not have recognized, who she was, if I had not spread, on her face, the breath of my words.

LVI

My body changes its skin, in front of the angel, who lends me some of his light, and takes the appearance of a slave, who shows me the path of ascension, we spin through the celestial houses, around the sun, eastern monarch, sitting, legs crossed, on his throne, then, we come back to earth, the angel disguises himself as a master, whom I guide, through cloudy weather, to a beach with white sand, strewn with pebbles, dry seaweed, tar, when we come near the convent, where the orantes sing, he disappears, without leaving a trace, which would have spared me torment.

LVII

Sometimes present, sometimes absent, I am not healed of ecstasy, of nostalgia, I meet her, I separate from her, when I am far away, I hope to see her, when I find her again, I am dizzy, the vision repeats itself, each time, greater, and the pain does not lessen.

LVIII

I walk through the remains of a noble palace, going toward the sandy river, I walk alongside a wire, is it a camp, is it a boundary, I am like a pile of dead leaves, that the rain wets, the drops of water fix the dust in place, and the day becomes brighter, and I, I keep my eyes open, after the pause in illness.

LIX

In fever, we met, in the desert, on the day, when the Jews rest, in the hollow of the red hill, near the water-filled crater, which casts a solitary banner, to the right of the trail, we shared desire, in the heart of noon, in the shade of a tent, we consumed, what we had accumulated, in pain, in snatches, in dreams, the time that speaks guided my steps, and hers, toward this ceasefire, which we left, translucent, like white flags flapping in the wind.

LX

Near the arborvitae, she told me, walk, you will arrive, do not trust sight, it is provisional, such is the law, when the tree moves, the shadow moves, I smelled the scent of the gazelle, which was panting and sweating, I went faster, to rejoin the night, which reunited us, and separated us, our greeting was our goodbye, I was enlightened, by the fire of the lady, who showed me the moon in flowers, before throwing stones, in the forbidden enclosure, she appeared to me, in her most beautiful form, then she retraced her steps, and blew out the flames, which had devoured the lion on my banner, she placed herself under the protection of fever, she surrounded herself with my ashen rags, she mended her broken wing, and undressed in the talons of the Falcon, which wanted to carry her off to his kingdom, over there, among black-sleeved dervishes, who grind the azure stone.

LXI

At the river's edge, in the shade of the willow, I hear the melody of the eagle wood, I breathe the wind, that sweeps the passage, burdened with timeworn objects, I stretch out my hand, from the table to the book, I touch the tree of light, I weave with my blood the black cloth, that covers the Cube, I spread the song of wormwood, on the smell of fuel oil, my palms are two paper lanterns, which gleam in the muted air of Mecca.

*These LXI stanzas were written between Paris and Tunis, from spring
to fall 1984, with a passionate energy, at that time in which revela-
tions, previously attributed to living gods, change into uncon-
conditional epiphanies, Aya inscribes her name on the notebooks of the betrothed who lead the song, in her actua-
lity, she revives the medieval Nidam, the young
Persian, elder sister of Beatrice, with whom Ibn
Arabi fell in love, in Mecca, in the year 598
of the Hegira, and who was the woman
who inspired his* Tarjuman al-Ashwaq,
*"The Interpreter of Ardent Desires,"
the divan in which certain motifs
travel from one shore to the other,
crossing centuries and languages, as if to accept the
celebration of love, the
source of movement,
without which the
universe would
be void.*

White Traverses

The washerwomen came to the house every Wednesday, the day of the week for the big wash, Bedouins from the plains and Berbers from the mountains, women with brown chins or with tattooed foreheads, crosses or brooches as if drawn with a stick of graphite, marks that didn't fade, didn't even trickle in the dewy flush of sweat: indelible, they folded into the tics and wrinkles that work inscribed on their skin, taut or flabby depending on age and the structure of the face.

Facing huge copper vats arranged on the paved area bordering the garden, between the washhouse and the shed, the washerwomen let themselves fall with all their weight, throwing their arms forward, then pulling them back: repeating their motions till they were in a trance, they kneaded the wash, beat it, rubbed it, twisted it, pulled it out, plunged it back into the sudsy liquid, activated by the dissolution of a royal-blue cube, foaming azure water that ran toward the drain later, after the rinsing and drying, when the vats were emptied.

Like boas curled at the bottom of these vessels with their tinned interiors, the pieces of laundry were brought out to dry in the area behind the house, the patio as adapted to the modern villa. Sheets, veils, shirts, *jebbas*[1] were spread, stretched before being fastened with wooden clothespins, hung from wire: expanses of white that the wind billowed out, made float, clatter: immaculate white, in the bright sunlight, where the spectrum made rainbows, evanescence of yellow and red flames, haunted by blue and green sparkles, immaterial debris where the mind could get lost.

Such visions I'm left with of all this white that came from the hands of the laundresses to dress the characters who peopled the scene of rituals in the city, like silhouettes of the veiled women on their way Fridays to visit the dead, scattering among the white patches of the tombs, punctuating as they moved, south out of Tunis, the many-colored hill in springtime, among the overgrown grasses and the sheaves of flowers, a dialogue that brings together the moving white of the veils and the fixed white of the tombs: intimate invocations, wordy confessions, women talking and singing, chased by the winged white of gulls escaped from the harbor, from the canal, or from the lake to perch on the crenellations of the Spanish fort that interrupts the harmony of white, an ocher crown where gray sparkles, set firmly on the crest of the hill, between sky and earth.

Or again in summer, at Mahdia, after twilight, on the esplanade that stretches past the quays, when there appeared to me as if by accident a troupe of men crowding out of the upper-class club, all dressed in *jebbas* blazing with whiteness, colony of seagulls, swarm of giant wood doves, moon banners bellied out by a favorable wind, sails scudding toward fresh watering holes, without hindrance or constraint, luminaries that lit up the night, whose rule was just beginning, ample whitenesses that let the air circulate in the intimacy of the body, ventilation that reverberated on the white of walls, white on white that softened the stay during the dog days' heat.

Should I add the hospitable whiteness of sheets that welcomed lovers during summer in the alcove of siesta? Salty bodies, tanned by the sun and the sea, burrowed beneath the profound penumbra of the white cave, delight sharpened in the multiplication of white: from top to bottom, from the curve to the right angle, from rigidity to suppleness, from the rough to the smooth, from the stucco to the weft, from stone to cloth.

Evening, between the visible and the tactile, between the eye and the touch, the smell of jasmines has insinuated itself, flowers gathered when the sun was starting its decline, in the last quarter of its course, closed petals whose undersides, Indian pink, tint of a fingernail, sealed the secret whiteness that illuminated the night with the addition of drunkenness, which it offered to lovers carried very high, toward their port of call on the moon.

In other seasons, other flowers wafted fragrance toward the opiated frontiers of the absolute, perhaps because of their whiteness, I think of orange blossoms, the flowers of citron, lemon trees, which diffused through the spring garden mute nighttime sonorities, which I caught and translated in my adolescent sleep into a psalm that drove my dream toward transgression, imagining myself in the act of violating my family's prohibition by manipulating the alembic that collected drop by drop the volatile spirit of the flowers in their evaporated whiteness, before I had to pass through anguish, expecting that family superstition would be confirmed and that death would pierce the walls of the house and come to inhale the soul of one of its residents.

I could recall other great washing sequences, in search of whiteness, feverish activity that would last for days picked during the hot season, almost at its peak, two or three weeks before *Awissou*, the month of the Julian calendar, the memory of whose Latin name was preserved in popular imagination, days spent in washing the newly gathered wool, undoing bundles of jute, bales larger than men, new wool arranged in heaps, sorted through in search of the prickly grains hidden there, wool from sheep that had just been shorn, not to be mixed up with wool that had already been used and that came from the unstitched and emptied-out mattresses, cushions, and pillows, yarn stuck together, tassels and fluff flattened and soaked in water, that the women trampled, collective dance increasing the intense animal smell, a choreography presented to me again outside, by the sea: at each strike of a heel, the peasant women's hips quivered under their turquoise *mélias*,[2] and their ankle bracelets jingled in the play of the rippling waves in which the sparkling of silver and foam was mixed, lunar gleams in the fiery noon, axis of day brought to the white heat they sometimes talk about in other idioms.

And I wonder: where should I wander to let the resonance of white resound in the endless progression of images I leaf through in the album of my memory?

"Whitening the wool," the washerwomen said, knowing that never would this substance attain immaculate whiteness, reflections of ivory veering to yellow that I found again with the animal smell in the burnous that the people of the Sahara wore indifferently summer and winter, half-white color that protected them from the sun in cold and warm months alike; that I found also in the robes of the Sufis, called *libden* ("body") and that disciples wore over their bare skin, so they could experience the Other body to body, electrified by the coarse wool, wool that absorbed the profuse sweat that practitioners and novices produced during their vaticinations in these sessions of *dhikr*, exercise that maintained awareness by means of chant and dance, to acquire His Presence by repeating *Huwa* till satiety, the two syllables of the third person pronoun that open onto the esplanade of Being, scansion of the loss of self, in the hope that by surprise the Absent might seize you by the tuft of hair that covered the nape of your neck, a knot called by metaphor *sufa*, signifying tuft of wool.

Thus lapses into ambiguity the etymology of the word *Sufi*, which wavers between Greek wisdom (*sophia*) and the reference to the Companions of the veranda (*soffa*)—the poor men who haunted the veranda onto which the house of the Prophet opened in Medina and who were raised to the status of founding heroes by the first Sufi generations—and between the wool of their robes (*suf*) or the tuft of hair (*sufa*) and the quest for purity (*safa*).

Not that I privilege the last option, but I grasp the opportunity of the connection that it creates to pause in the shelter of its station and recall that purity haunts the color white and induces the effect expected from the act of washing. I remember the pathetic search of Abu Yazid, the Iranian Sufi of the ninth century who lived in Bestam, not far from the Elburz Mountains and the Caspian Sea, and who said (I quote from memory): "For twenty years I was a washerman [*blanchisseur*] and I never reached purity."

This purity will always escape, it is an infinite, unfulfilled, impossible quest: the whitest white will hide itself from purity, and it is in its brilliance that we want to track it down and enjoy its illusion, pretending to forget that into the purest whiteness the potentiality for stains insinuates itself.

I think of another saying uttered by the ecstatic from Bestam whose mouth was overflowing with raptures, like a river in spate; his inspired paradoxes streamed forth from enthusiastic lips, like grains that spurt from the circumductions of the millstone, scattering out from the orifice of the axle and through the gap between the two stones. Phrases of excess aroused by what Jean-Jacques would have called poetic and musical oestrus, leaving us haggard-faced with their actual ambivalences. Addressing himself in the second person, Abu Yazid is supposed to have said: "Women are pure once a month, twice perhaps; yet you, oh self, never have you been able to leave the impure state!" As long as the stain remains a potentiality, purity is preserved; when it is inscribed and then erased, then purity is won. It is even celebrated after the female subject painfully rids herself of the residues that her blood flushes out, a supplementary operation that does not apply to the economy of the male subject. It is this inversion of common opinion that Abu Yazid disseminated twice from the height of his asexuality, according to a paradoxical inspiration in which self-hatred probably figured. And if the reader likens the physical stain to the moral stain, he might infer that this exclusively feminine operation imposes a morality erected on considerations of health and body. No stronger foundations for the moral edifice, Nietzsche might have joyfully exclaimed!

When I was a child, might I have confusedly witnessed this arrival of purity by means of the impure through the rags and napkins that women used to contain the blood of their periods, especially when these squares of sponge-cloth were washed and set out to dry in the sun in their often rediscovered whiteness, sometimes still marked by wine-colored aureoles or streaks?

And what of the traces of the torn hymen, signs of blood that were exhibited in the countryside on the white sheets the day after the wedding to proclaim the inaugural as conceived by the patriarchal archaic perennial myth of virginity? I cannot believe that this physiological transformation was involved in the quest for the pure. It is a wound inviting the experience of pain within pleasure: I mention it because it shows a mark, as if to recall that whiteness hungers for stains, preferably blood.

It is surprising to note the convergence between the language in which I write and these images from a past infiltrated by the murmur of another tongue. The alloglot imagination corroborates this written language, which registers in some of its phrases this disposition of the color white to accompany blood:

the two languages link together to offer diverse significations established either on the strength of the meaning itself or through the license of metaphor. As when one says of the timid by hyperbole that "he blushed to the white of his eyes." Or in the expression "white weapons" [*armes blanches*, knives], sharpened blades that gleam, wound, and sometimes cut to the quick until the blood has run dry. Or in the metaphor "to bleed someone white," which echoes older phrases, like "turned white" [*mettre au blanc*] or "reduced to white" [*réduire à blanc*], used in previous centuries to describe a ruined person. And from the metaphoric use that these expressions occasioned one came closer to the literal association when circumstances invited the saying "he bled him white," meaning to exhaustion.

So white amounts to bloodless. And blood while it colors cheerful faces remains the sign of life. When one considers the body from the inside, white, the symbol of purity, meets the curve of entropy if not of death (don't we say "white as a corpse"?) and blood, which is exteriorized in the fleck, in the stain, is what irrigates life: as long as it remains invisible, it drains its flow into the network of veins and gives a ruddy aura to faces overflowing with vitality. It is as if the principle of life were governed by that which, imposing itself on white, symbolizes the impure. That is the inversion this symbolism approaches when it opposes white with blood.

And as far as blood itself goes, it is clear that the symbol mutates and adapts itself to its opposite. Everything depends on the path that it takes. Did not the Son of Man say, "Drink ye, this is my blood"? In the circularity of the symbol, in its intricate transferrals and metamorphoses, negative and positive are scarcely mutually exclusive. One lingers in the memory of the other. The impure marks the pure. That is the ambivalence to which we are led by the meditation centered on opposites we have succeeded in mixing, but that prescriptive Reason might prefer us to experience in their unchangeability.

If such a contrast is sufficiently striking to act on the intricacies of language, nothing keeps it from tracing a horizon for the symbolic universe. Thus we find again in esoteric poetry that association of red and white, the color of blood and of immaculate whiteness. As with Dante, who reminds us at the beginning of *Vita Nuova* that when he saw her for the first time when she was nine, Beatrice wore a blood-red dress, and that at the second meeting, nine years later, she was dressed in the whitest color; and, as if intoxicated by the inaugural word that the most noble lady spoke to him in the street, he detached himself from the crowd to withdraw to his room, where, dozing, he saw in a dream Beatrice naked surrounded by a light sheet the color of blood, and carried by the Lord of Love, who gave her the poet's heart consumed by flames to devour. If, in this context, whiteness naturally symbolizes purity (and faith), love makes the color of blood come to it (symbol of caritas) to transfigure its stain, and purify it in turn by the ardor of fire.

To return to white, receptacle of stains and scraps, I again draw from the reserve of childhood, and, in my evocation, I move to the other sex in extracting from my memory the *bissa*, the turban that enveloped the phallus of fathers, in their desperate search for canonical purity, in their concern bordering on mania to rid themselves of the least excremental remainder, the *bissa* being a kind of handkerchief that attaches a rectangle to a triangle extended at its tip by a long string; with such a cloth one surrounded the circumcised glans to collect the minute liquid emanation that might persist after the scrupulous ablutions made after each urination. The term *bissa*, which designates this cloth, is an interjection in Arabic signifying ill fortune. Through less obvious if not diaphanous stains, white joins in to control the evil part: it's through the purity of white that one attempts to track down the impure drops at the tip of the phallus! I would come upon these handkerchiefs while they were drying, immaculate, next to the menstrual rags, a way of demonstrating the difference between the sexes through the white accessories that fluttered there.

It seems a great effort, if one hadn't seen it, to imagine the white stain on the white background, white on white, colorless stains that sometimes veered toward light rings tinted with citrine shades, like the marks of what for women are called "white losses" [vaginal discharge] and that the menstrual rags sometimes collected; or for men the accidental seminal discharges, whose fate was to be absorbed by the *bissa*.

Interrupting the transcription of this visionary evocation of the past, I go out for a walk in Paris. Heading toward the hills of Père Lachaise, I dawdle along the Rue de la Roquette; after looking over the square that has replaced the women's prison, my attention is drawn to an abandoned store; on its front is written in large letters *Maison du Blanc* [House of White]. I figure that it's in shops bearing such names that one stocks up on white goods, pieces to be subjected as the days go by to the drama of purity and defilement that in my childhood provoked a ceremony initiating a monumental domestic drama made possible by the distinction created by a belief endlessly renewed by feminine servile compliance.

Entering the cemetery, climbing the steps of the hill, feeling the roughness of the pavement, which touches sensitive points awakening from the flow of energy rising from the soles of my feet toward the rest of my body after having been caught up in the channels that run along my shins, I brush by the tomb of Musset, which is still not shaded by the song of the weeping willow the poet asked for in his epitaph; and the first sight I ever had of snow comes to mind when, a unique event, it had fallen in Tunis: I was ten years old, it was a Friday, and I was dazzled by this white cloak that had covered the familiar scene; I walked in the garden's paths; each of my steps left a trace that stained the white uniformity; since the snowfall did not continue, very quickly these traces changed into puddles of mud. Since then, when confronting snowy landscapes, I again feel the certainty that purity does not belong to our condition: Isn't every human passage a stain? You have only to exert yourself in the apprenticeship that teaches you to dance as you walk, carrying your body in an airy gait that promises to weaken the inscription of a stain, and whose quickness will not aggravate the turbulence that seizes the face of the earth each time you start moving.

In my notebooks and on my glowing screen, I test the analogy of snow offering the contrast of a white continuity into which clearly perceptible traces are inlaid. I try out this analogy on a more intense level in the act of writing, which stains the white page or the screen of light with signs that change color (blues, reds, sepia, etc.) and that are gathered under the call of black. It's not that I want to negate myself and return to the privilege of silence and nonaction, but I am devoted to not hiding from the knowledge of evil, so that I can be ready to curb it when it assails me in my deeds. And I continue the prophylaxis that accompanies the position of the scribe with an invitation to take the passage that leads to my secret black-on-white site. This is the extent of the act of witness that grounds the pact of writing: it is in the cult of the stain, the very thing that encourages me to blacken the pages, to put the black on the white, to use the conventional expression[3] with its archaic particles that strengthen its meaning through the determinacy added by the definite article.

It is to ward off the primacy of the impure, of the stain, of evil, that Islam, in whose shadow I grew up, urges its adherents to privilege white as much in the exaltation of its fictions as in the ardor of its practices.

Before coming to these fictions and practices, I will recall that Islam establishes white as a fixed mark of astronomical observation, criterion of the ritual that gives believers an awareness of a metric in harmony with the music of the spheres. As in the detection, by the naked eye, of the first glimpse of the new moon that announces the beginning of Ramadan, the month that contains the Night of Destiny, which, according to the scriptures, is better than a thousand months. One must be able to capture the furtive appearance of the orb, reduced to a white hair whose inscription lasts for only a brief instant nested in the final, still-white hours of daylight. In order to be up to this task, a gaze of steel must quicken the searcher's eye so that it can grasp this white, tenuous as a thread of silver sketched on the white plate of day. Similarly, his gaze must extract the first isolated white thread of the nocturnal weft, which precedes the initial gleams of dawn at the end of a night that has still not emerged from its darkness: at that second the satisfaction of the senses ceases, and the sacred time of abstinence begins, which will extend until the return of the profane hours that follow upon evening twilight.

By the division of that astronomical reference mark, the ritual examines, in the lodges of the sky, two occurrences that we have already experienced: that of the white sign inscribed on the white ground, and that of the contrast the combination of white and black introduces. Magnified then on the cosmic scale is the symbolism that accords white the benefit of purity, since it is the white sign that announces sacred time through launching the month and hours devoted to the purifying fast. In projecting the myth of this sacred time allied with white, the practitioner, whose duty is to suspend the exteriorization of the stain that accompanies his deeds, the black smudge, the evil that lurks in every whiteness, experiences his discipline.

And the astrological celebration of white is rendered even more immanent by the fable that flourishes behind the scenes where the communal meal took place honoring the day of the Hegiran year; then, as children, we were invited the next day to find in the nighttime portion of the ritual couscous the white hair that two priests come from the secret world offer to the moon for the variation of its whiteness, between waxing and waning, flood and ebb, necessary for the rolling onward of months on the wheel of the circle that encloses the year. This marrowy, salty couscous is subject to the law of a recipe I imagine is very old: on the threshold of History, it may have beèn served at the triclinia that accommodated the funeral banquets where the pact of the clan was renewed. I like to detect in it a pagan origin adopted by monotheist belief. A part of the dish is reserved for the ghosts of the old man and the old woman; in the darkness, this portion, which lasts the night, will have caught the white hair from one of the two phantoms who leaned over it to steep itself in an earthly scent emanating from the ingredients reserved and offered for the cooking, semolina of cracked wheat, dried beans, and preserved meat (*qaddid*), from the head of the lamb sacrificed twenty days earlier on the altar renewed to commemorate and imitate the Abrahamic gesture.

It is neither simple chance nor simple conformity to Mediterranean practice, this tendency to whitewash all the places that shelter the sacrificial energy that the cult of saints in Africa channels, temples in the shape of squat domes, which are called by metonymy *marabouts*, and which are scattered throughout the countryside, occupying the most beautiful sites, in a preoccupation with eminences that leads them to capture hillocks and mounds in a low-lying country. Is this the only concern about the site that led these sacred foundations to share closeness with Roman foundations and other ancient remains? Not at all: the rites and pilgrimages that these places keep alive are indebted to a persistence of shamanism. So rise up those white banners of popular faith, a place of cure for stricken souls, whose bare white walls are like sheets of paper and stelae greedy to receive the feverish graffiti that visitors and travelers trace with the help of a rod dipped in a bowl of henna, white stained by the signs of their sickness of being and of love. A gesture that leaves them with a confused premonition that purity is not of this world, and that their participation in being-there begins with welcoming the stain and with the injunction of the impure.

The propensity to whiten was not the prerogative only of that vernacular architecture where traces of living shamanism are sheltered. Monuments as prestigious and orthodox as the great Aghlabid Mosque of Kairouan (which dates from the ninth century) were whitewashed throughout all their parts before the hypostyle hall, the cortile portico, the surrounding wall, and the doors were stripped and adapted to the current taste, which privileges the pleasure of structure laid bare. Whiteness haunted by stain suggests a nice similarity with the aniconism of Islamic tradition, haunted in its turn by projection into the sensory of the mental icon. Every image comes from above, and it acquires its reality only when it shines forth into the realm of the impure. And whiteness is nothing if not this desperate quest that does its utmost to prevent the emergence of the image, in the wake of the impure, where life palpitates.

Thus it is no accident that this whiteness is found to be pervasive in the sanctuaries that dot the insular landscape of Djerba, chosen dwelling place of the sect of Ibadites, a small minority of living witnesses from Islam's most ancient schism, arisen scarcely a generation after its birth. These rigorist Kharijites, of hereditary doctrinal austerity, built, between the monumental and the vernacular, mosques that are, from the ground to their heights, completely coated with whitewash. It is an architecture where plaster takes over to accommodate shapes molded like sculpture, bearing in their excrescences an approximation to the sense of proportion the human hand creates. Between the embossing and the distribution of the masses sometimes emerges an apse for a mihrab, sometimes a retaining angle where the image of a circumcised phallus can be made out, sometimes a succession of flying buttresses that offer a perspective on a portico, sometimes the apposition of an oblique vestibule where the steps of a staircase climb right up to the wall as if to give access to an invisible throne.

I will not forget the tomb that is built into the ground, into the wall, in a sheath of whiteness: nothing distinguishes it except the subtle lines that reveal its shape and that the surface barely separates from the site where it is embedded. Evanescent tomb, as if to celebrate the memory of a volatile soul. What grants it existence more than any other attribute is perhaps the post from which a lamp hangs at foot level, sign of the female identity of the remains buried there. A post that, in the identification of the tomb, competes with the tombstone, which, in its broken and ogival profile, pours forth the rolling, ample letters that the *ta'liq* style commands, very common in Persia, in the Orient, a sign that the sponsor has traveled; white letters on white ground, as if to obviate any last appeal to the analogy between writing and stain: the stain is lessened, even annulled, when whiteness absorbs whiteness in an equality that demands recourse to something else, the effect of the raised relief, to establish a starting point for decipherment.

Whiteness that follows the cycle of the seasons: it cracks in summer, flakes in autumn, becomes decrepit in winter; and in spring its luster is renewed.

Then, as protection and propitiation, it shines under the African sun as if to chase away crime and evil from the landscape. The desperate quest begins for the religious absolute whose immanence establishes a paradox: its presence tempers the temptation of transgression while, in the same spirit, it invites blasphemy. This whiteness, in short, you run into wherever you turn: perhaps it acts like a series of signals supposed to define the path of the moral subject; perhaps it quickens, without meaning to, the desire for overindulgence and excess.

Whiteness of light is the condition of clear sight, but its intensity blinds and veils. It creates that blurred space where the angel appears, himself clothed all in white, in Pasolini's Annunciation in the *Gospel of Matthew*, as well as in Mohammed's vision in which the same angel transforms into a beautiful foreign youth come to sit down in the circle of Meccan and Medinan Companions without anyone recognizing him; after his departure, the Prophet reveals to them: "Gabriel was among you and I spoke with him in secret; he asked me: 'What is Doing Right?' I answered him: 'It is adoring God as if you saw him and if you do not see him, he sees you.'" This is a tradition that lends legitimacy to the mental icon, which is realized in the mode of *as if*, which founds the aesthetics of likeness. And which will come to haunt the empty walls of sanctuaries like the stain that hovers around whiteness. And which will help the subject to internalize a way of bypassing the obstacle that blocks the occurrence of the impure, in the heart of life.

Finally I come to the Night Journey and the Ascension of the Prophet, which in the imagination of poets and mystics gave life to so many legends, and narrative embellishments adorning so many works, one of them *The Book of the Ladder*, which, in its peregrinations through languages, from Arabic to Spanish to Latin to Old French, carried its murmurings all the way to the ears of Dante, to lend some of its structure and imagery to the composition of the *Divine Comedy*. Rereading one of the sequences in that book (chapter 52), I find an additional confirmation of the hegemony of white among the symbols of Islam. Of all the beverages contained in the beautiful vases that the angel Ridohan, guardian of Paradise, offered him to drink, the Prophet drank all of the one that tasted like milk and rejected with horror the one that resembled wine in its taste and smell. By refusing the wine, the red stain, the divine blood, the impurity and drunkenness encountered on the paths of life, and by accepting the milky diet, which sustains the fantasy of purity and the innocence of lactation that follows childbirth, a whiteness supporting one of the mysteries that our coming into the world provokes, the Prophet delayed the increase of delights promised to his community by the angel Gabriel at the very beginning of the celestial ascension.

Is it for the role it plays in nurture that Tradition interprets milk as a symbol of science? Unless a section of the veil is raised from this science, where does a knowledge dwell that is destined to banish the impure reality of the world and of life by offering in compensation this double of absolute lactescence? Still, the Mohammedan community, in its turbulent fringes, from the dregs and from the heights, did not conform to the preference of its founder: moved by the vital spirit of the impure, poets, profane and holy, allusive and explicit, upheld the great transgression of Islam by directing their creative energy toward the dense bacchic divan where the praise of wine was transcribed in the spirit of a fugue, in which tones and overtones follow each other. They didn't have to shun the taverns and wine cellars, these fearless ones who don't have to wait for the beatific life in Paradise to stagger under the effects of the divine fluid, entering the mouth like a metaphor or like the daughter of the vine.

Coming to the end of this meditation, I notice that the language in which I am writing—French—enriches the metaphors for white by neutralizing it, by associating it with the negative and with evil. In this area, I survey two other ranges of images and meanings, some of whose echoes I do not want to silence, even at the risk of rambling or seeming out of place. The first range includes shadowy activities, like the white slave trade or trafficking in the white lady, whose profits bring dirty money that goes through processes of laundering [*blanchiment*] (this metaphoric usage can also be made positive when it is applied to a person who has been sullied by accusations and who is "cleared" [*blanchi*] if he is vindicated). The second range of meanings associates fruitless deeds with white, like a paper marriage [*mariage blanc*] (which was not consummated) or a "white wind" (which is not followed by rain), or firing with blank cartridges [*tir à blanc*].

When I return to my first language—Arabic—I find white, antonym of black, buffeted by ambivalences that do not repudiate either sin or the negative. Opening a lexicon of medieval Arabic, traces of which still are found in common usage, I travel through the text that covers the root letters *b.y.dh.* from which white is derived; there I discover opposite orientations: the equivalent of "to whiten" alternates between brilliance and setting things straight; a twofold direction illustrated by various contexts: like painting, daubing in white and copying from the rough draft to the clean copy; or blinding and exterminating, annihilating; or again, at the height of contradiction, both filling and emptying a utensil (with white liquids, like water and milk). I gather some metaphors that bloom in the garden of this root where I see that the white hand slides from kind deed to power, from ability to glory; that days of whiteness are those that are prolonged by the three nights when the moonlight is brightest; that white earth is earth that is empty, as if it had not been blackened by cultivation or by signs of human habitation; that white lends its name as much to the sun as to the sword and to money; that along with milk and water, the two whites of fat and bread are added to mingle their pairs; that white by itself invokes calamity, misfortune; that "white death" is the announcement of sudden death; and that the wearing of exclusively white clothes classifies you among those who have dedicated themselves to death.

Perhaps it is because of this irreducibility of evil and the negative that white has been sublimated by the fiction of the pure. This fiction has made us companions of white from cradle to tomb, from our swaddling clothes to the shroud.

Whether I reconsider my past, whether I question my first language or my language of writing, I notice that white contains so many possibilities, that it summons to itself good and evil, life and death, that it entrains a series of opposites: Isn't it pure virtuality? Truly, white is the most beautiful metaphor for God. Listen to Ramon Lull: "The white circle is the only one whose surface is not divided. It contains in potentiality many unities, that is lines, measures and figures of succeeding circles. Similarly . . . we say that, just as the white circle is the principle of the other circles, so, and even better, God is the simple principle, containing in him substantially, actually, and naturally many simple unities" (*Principles and Questions of Theology*). Through this metaphor circumscribed on the white (that is to say empty) circle, Lull illustrates the first principle of his *Ars Generalis Ultima*, whose aim was to confound in their belief those whom he calls the Saracens and to convince them to join his own belief. If he had grasped the immanence of white, meaning God, in the life of Islam, he would surely have spared himself the burden of such an insane project.

Paris, October 1996

Afterword
Three Questions about *Tombeau of Ibn Arabi*

JEAN-LUC NANCY

I have been asked to write an "afterword." One ought to be silent, though, when the poem is over. At the most, even furtively, I might ask three questions, ones that the reader, like me, will have found reading this text necessarily leads to, letting the questions show through though without ever being willing to ask them.

1. What is a *tombeau*?

A *tombeau* is a poetic genre invented in the Renaissance to celebrate a dead person, often first collectively, then individually. The poetic genre at times has had emulators in music (Ravel's "Tombeau de Couperin"). Among the Moderns, Mallarmé gave a unique touch to the genre with the "Tombeau d'Edgar Poe," which is nothing other than a funeral celebration of the *Poëte* in himself and for himself.

Funeral? Yes, since the *tombeau* is posthumous, that goes without saying. But "funeral" not primarily, and perhaps not at all, in the sense of mourning, affliction, threnody, or lamentation. In the *tombeau*, one does not regret, one celebrates instead.

Of the funerary monument the poetic genre retains the monument more than the funerary. More precisely: of the funerary it retains the monumental quality it always has, that is to say, it retains the *eternity* by which the dead person *in himself* is *changed*. It stands in the immortal presence of death. The dead person's death is not forgotten: it is magnified within it like the seal forever imprinted on a name and by that name itself. The *tombeau* guards the dead person, takes him away from his death, presents him to the living.

Poe, through his "Tombeau," becomes the *Poëte*. Ibn Arabi, by the *Tombeau* that Meddeb raises, becomes the lover who eternally *enters into pleasure* [jouissance].

Eternally: think about this well. It does not mean "perpetually." It does not speak of an endless beginning again: it speaks of a beginning removed from the time of beginning and succession. The eternal encloses the simultaneity of all successions. Here, in this *tombeau*, outside of chronic time, beats the rhythmic time of a pleasure "like white sheets beaten by the wind."

The *tombeau* is rhythm: scansion of presence and passage. Here, this is the step that leads from *entering into pleasure* to no exit but only to this *white footstep that weakens the ground*, a step that seeks nothing more, a step suspended in this infinite imminence that is called joy.

2. Who is speaking?

His last words are uttered in Mecca. That is the present of the poem, and the note tells us that it is Year 598 of the Hegira. It is Ibn Arabi speaking. It is he who speaks with the voice of Meddeb. He, Meddeb, is far from Mecca. Far from and turned toward it, toward the precise Mecca of 598 where the Poet, the Thinker, the Sufi falls in love with and enters into pleasure. Turned toward it from all the distance of his exile. Keeping that distance. *Traveling in time* as well as *in the world where solitude begins and ends*,

Meddeb uses the voice of one to whom he gives his own. Voice split in two like these *two letters that are mirrored in my name*.

(Learn how to say this name: *med-deb*, note well the caesura, the tonguing of it.)

From the *tombeau*, he makes his place. He nourishes no fantasy of identification or split personality. Ibn Arabi is not reincarnated in him. But he knows that there is one single voice. One single voice whose solitude shuts down and opens up at the same time. A voice from beyond the grave, a voice from beyond the world, but a voice of this world, fervent echo of *the beautiful Arab with the Latin voice*.

It is always one single, same voice—worldly, worldwide, hoping for a world? which loves and takes pleasure, which summons and *which celebrates beauty*, even when he must do so *among a destitute people*. The one speaking here strains toward the unique voice, toward the immortal timbre of a song that could be taken up from east to west, from home to exile and again finding a home at the end of exile—in order to leave from there again and always to return toward *the black cloth that covers the Cube*.

Like the lady *dressed in the color black*, the *Cube* shelters a profuse, hidden presence, revealed as a secret, fervent, inexhaustible. The presence of one who speaks: the Arab, wandering, *neither from the east, nor from the west*.

3. Comma?

You wonder what these commas are, what they do.

There is no punctuation other than commas, throughout the single sentence that makes up each stanza and that ends with a period (sometimes a question mark). There is no punctuation other than commas, but they are deployed quite differently from the way the syntactic usage of this punctuation proposes, that is, a slight suspension, intended to articulate a subordinate proposition or else an interpolated clause – but not at all to separate a verb from its object or a word from its relative pronoun. To take an example particularly resonant for the French reader:

no one dares come near, beyond the principle, which demands to be kept in.

Comma, little wand, little branch, bar—almost a *slash*, really, but the latter brackets together by separating, whereas the comma opens nothing but a distance in liaison, a slight suspension in the sequence. The period interrupts, the comma gives rhythm to the flow—but rhythm here according to a manifest principle of scansion, of breath, foreign to the rhythm of syntax.

It is another rhythm that beats in language without dismembering it, as line endings would do, which would be easy to imagine here as replacements for the commas, and which would arrange the text into free verse.

But he does not want this explicit, printed invitation to follow a prosody. He insinuates into the continuous sentence, supposedly prose, always going in front of itself—*prorsa*—these little wings, these tiny paws or claws that at first you don't notice, accustomed as you are to their presence in language (English, in this case, which will certainly have given some anxiety to the translator), but that soon you begin to find incongruous, even to suspect of being erroneous, before you understand that they dance a counterpoint [*contre-pas*] to the gait [*pas*] of the stanza. They catch you off-balance, keep you in place when you were stepping over—but not always, and that is the secret: not always the misstep, since often too the comma is just in its place, ordinary, ingenuous, whereas often elsewhere it is tricky, displaced. So you stumble over them, at every step, you never know if you're still underway or if you have to watch your step, even take a detour.

Thus: *I enter into the black, of her black eyes.*[1]

Do you read this as "I enter into the black of her black eyes"? Or "Starting from her black eyes I enter into the black"?

You don't know, that alone is certain: you enter with him into the dark.

Notes

Preface

1. *The Tarjuman al-Ashwaq: A Collection of Mystical Odes*, by Muhyi'ddîn Ibn al-'Arabî, trans. Reynold A. Nicholson (London: Royal Asiatic Society, 1911). The title means "The Interpreter of Desire."

White Traverses

1. The *jebba*, a specifically Tunisian garment, is an ample robe worn by men, falling to mid-calf, worn over baggy pants. A deep slit in the chest of the *jebba* reveals the shirt and vest worn underneath. In winter, a burnous is worn over the jebba.—Trans.

2. A *mélia* is the brightly colored tunic worn by Bedouins over bare skin.—Trans.

3. Meddeb here changes the usual *noir sur blanc* ("black on white") to the older expression *du noir sur du blanc*, using the definite articles.— Trans.

Afterword

1. *De ses yeux noirs* could be translated either as "of her black eyes" or "from her black eyes."—Trans.